MARGRET & H. A. REY'S

# Happy Easter, Curious George

*Written by* R. P. Anderson

*illustrated in the style of* H. A. Rey *by* Mary O'Keefe Young

Houghton Mifflin Harcourt
Boston  New York

www.hmhbooks.com

The text of this book is set in Adobe Garamond Pro.

Library of Congress Cataloging-in-Publication Data Control Number 2008040468

ISBN: 978-0-547-04825-3

Manufactured in China
LEO 10 9 8 7 6 5 4

4500274502

This is George.
He was a good little monkey and always very curious.
He lived with his friend, the man with the yellow hat.
Today George and the man were going to the park as a special treat.

George was curious the moment they got to the park.
It was Easter, and the park was full of people!

There were so many bright colors and
so many things for a little monkey to do.

Children were flying kites high in the sky and decorating Easter baskets. They were even having races rolling eggs.

Then George saw a small corral with a sign on it. What could be inside?

A soft white bunny! He patted the bunny and fed it a carrot.

But—what was this?

People were dyeing Easter eggs yellow and blue and pink.

George was curious. He had never dyed an egg before.

George dyed an egg yellow.

Then George had an idea.

With yellow and red
he made orange,

with yellow and blue
he made green,

and with red and blue
he made purple!

He dyed eggs as only a monkey can — four at a time!

Then he painted the eggs with swirls, with polka dots, and with stars.

They looked like brightly colored balls! George could not resist— he even juggled them.

"Oh, no!" shouted a woman.
"The Easter Bunny is gone!"

But George didn't notice
because just then he saw
a man losing one egg,

then another egg,

and then even more eggs.

In an instant, George
grabbed a basket

and began to help
the man find them.

George found eggs here and he found eggs there.
He had almost collected them all when a boy
said, "Hey, that monkey's taking the Easter eggs!
Stop, thief!"

George was so busy that he did not even hear him.
Then he saw another egg! A white egg under some
bushes, perfect for dyeing.

It wasn't an egg at all! It was a bunny's tail.

How surprised George was. He patted the bunny
and placed it in his basket on top of the eggs.

"Hey, that monkey found the Easter Bunny!" said a girl.
"Hurrah!" cried a boy.
Everyone congratulated George.

"Now that the Easter Bunny is safe and sound, George,"
said the man with the yellow hat, "can you hide all of
the eggs you gathered so the children can find them?"

For this job, he was lucky
to be a monkey. George hid
the eggs in all the places a
curious monkey would.

It was the best egg hunt ever!

After the hunt, George and the man with the
yellow hat waved goodbye to their new friends.

As George and his friend drove away, the children
waved back, calling out, "Happy Easter, George!"